The Prepper's Guide To Grid Down Survival

How To Prepare, Survive And Become Self Reliant If The Lights Go Out & The Water, Gas Or Energy Grid Collapses

By Ron Johnson

Contents

Introduction

Introduction

You can try and predict a hundred different scenarios about what the future may hold, but it is almost impossible to do so. Your best bet is to create an umbrella of preparation. Cover all of your bases and you will feel better and fare better. One of the things preppers plan for is an act of terror that will disrupt our way of lives. It isn't always only a bomb or a plane hitting a building that is considered an act of terror. In fact, a more plausible event is a terrorist attack which takes out the power grid.

Could you survive if the power grid suffered a major failure? What if the failure lasted days, weeks, months, or even years? This is a situation that the United States government knows can happen. They have been running drills and prepping emergency responders for a major power grid failure.

Are you secure enough to trust in our government's ability to provide for you and your family during the interim? Will you feel safe? Can you keep your family safe when things are chaotic? Will the government be able to provide security when there is civil unrest disrupting the streets?

These are questions that you can't take a "wait-and-see" approach. You need to take action now to ensure that will keep your family safe and healthy in the aftermath of a grid failure.

Chapter 1
Possible Causes of a Grid Down and Why You Should Be Prepared

Are you still sceptical about the idea that a grid could ever fail? There are several different scenarios that could result in a power grid failure. A major failure would have a trickle-down effect that would result in a failure of the water supply system. Natural gas lines could also fail, leaving the country paralysed and freezing for those who rely on gas to run the house's furnace.

The following are some of the most plausible causes of a major grid failure:

- A nuclear weapon doesn't only pose a risk to human health. In fact, a nuclear weapon doesn't even have to be detonated close to the earth's surface to cause significant damage. A small nuclear bomb which exploded in the earth's atmosphere would create an electromagnetic pulse that would disrupt the power grid. A single blast could take out half the country in a matter of seconds.

- A computer hacker or well-executed virus could destroy the power grid. This is a very real possibility and could damage the system all across the country. The

```
0 00 00-6D 73 62 6C            msbl
0 6A 75-73 74 20 77    ast.exe I just w
9 20 4C-4F 56 45 20    ant to say LOVE
0 62 69-6C 6C 79 20    YOU SAN!! billy
0 64 6F-20 79 6F 75    gates why do you
3 20 70-6F 73 73 69     make this possi
0 20 6D-61 6B 69 6E    ble ? Stop makin
E 64 20-66 69 78 20    g money and fix
7 61 72-65 21 21 00    your software!!
0 00 00-7F 00 00 00
0 00 00-01 00 01 00
0 00 00-00 00 00 46
C C9 11-9F E8 08 00
0 00 03-10 00 00 00
0 00 00-01 00 04 00
```

threat of a virus infiltrating our power systems is only half the battle. A virus could shut down our communication systems, banking systems, and even transportation systems. This scenario has already happened on a much smaller scale. This could have just been the warm up for what's to come.

- A solar flare could also release an electromagnetic pulse (EMP) that would knock out the power systems. There are thousands of flares that happen every day. Those flares are fairly small and don't pose any real problems. There have been large solar flares in the past that have interrupted satellite systems, but even those were minor compared to what the sun could do. One scientist feels the threat of massive solar flare is more likely than the threat of a nuclear bomb causing a similar-sized EMP.

- A physical attack on numerous power stations at one time could also wreak havoc on the main power grid. This scenario has already happened, but on a small scale. If a coordinated attack was instigated, it could cause a massive grid failure. The attack could be devastating and take several months from which to recover.

- A natural disaster that takes down the power grid is a real possibility. Think back to the Fukushima disaster. An earthquake set off a chain of events that had cataclysmic effects.

Above: The Fukushima nuclear disaster of 2011 is probably the most well known incident where natural disaster caused a major grid failure

These are just some of the scenarios that could happen. You don't need to be a conspiracy theorist to have these beliefs. It doesn't take much to prepare for this situation. Taking the time to prepare today could keep your family alive tomorrow.

Chapter 2
What May Happen If the Grid Collapses in the Short Term

If the reason for the grid collapse was that it was caused by something minor, there is a good chance the grid will only be down for a short amount of time. Short-term is still plenty of time for things to get a little unsafe; Short term can be defined by power being out for weeks or even months. Going even 24 hours without electricity is pretty tough, especially if you are not adequately prepared.

Some things that can be expected to happen in a short-term grid collapse are as follows:

- Incessant darkness may not seem like a big deal right now, but when you are forced to live in the darkness for days at a time, it can become suffocating. You don't fully understand the scope of complete darkness until street lights are taken away, porch lights or even those annoying security lights. If it is a cloudy night, you won't even have the moon to help you see. The darkness can make people a little crazy. You need a way to break it up to make you feel safer as well as offer a sense of comfort and normalcy.

- The water supply will run dry within days. Without power, main water supply systems cannot properly clean and filter your drinking water. If you have your own well, you won't have electricity to run your pump. Without clean water, the fight will be intense as people scramble to get the liquid that is absolutely necessary for survival.

- People will be fighting to stay warm if the power grid failure happens during the winter or in cold parts of the world. That means people will be fighting for blankets, warm clothing, and things to burn to stay warm. Keeping the family warm will be a priority that people will be willing to fight for.

- Food will become scarce within days of the power grid failure. Grocery store shelves will be wiped out with no immediate plan for restocking and reopening the store will wait until the power grid is back up. Although humans can technically go weeks without eating, nobody wants to and there will be fights to the death as people scramble to find food.

These are just some of the things that will happen, even in a short-term power grid collapse. Gas stations will be offline, which means there will be no gas to put in your car to travel to find food, water, and other supplies. Although there will be an end in sight, it is hard to see the forest through the trees so to speak. The future may not be quite as grim compared to a long-term collapse, but people are going to struggle to see that. It is going to consist of every person living in the moment. People are going to struggle to get through every hour of the day without power if they are filled with fear.

Chapter 3
How to Prepare for Limited Access to Running Water

Your biggest concern, aside from staying warm and out of the elements of nature, will be obtaining water. You need water to survive. The human body can only go three days without water. However, after just a single day of no clean drinking water, your health will suffer. Dehydration won't kill you instantly. It starts out with some subtle warning signs, like a headache, before it slowly starts causing you problems that will leave you completely incapacitated.

If you can only store one item in your home, it should be water. Along with the water, a way to clean and purify it should also be readily available.

There are numerous options available for you to use in order to store water. The more water stored the better. Don't skimp on water storage! Go out of your way to create a water storage plan.

Check out some of the following ways you can store water in your home in case of a failed power grid:

- Rain barrels are an effective way to store water and they are extremely inexpensive. It is also an excellent way to replenish your water supply just in case you go through your water before the grid  failure is over. You can make the rain barrels yourself for under $10 or so. If you don't want to make one or two, you can buy them ready made.

- Cisterns that you will often see at farm supply stores are another great option if you have your own land. These large vessels are perfect for storing large amounts of water. You will need to fill the vessel, which can take a while if you are using your current water supply. You can also supplement the cistern's water supply by creating a rain catchment system. This is a great way to replenish your water supply throughout the duration of a grid failure.

- Bottled water is always an option. However, it can get pricey. If you have the funds and can afford to spend the money buying bottled water, go for it. Keep in mind, each family member will need a gallon of water per day. That is a lot of bottled water. You can bottle your own water, but choose plastics that are BPA free and are a heavy-weight plastic, like soda bottles. Don't use milk jugs. They are made of a thin plastic that will break

down in a matter of weeks. Jars are also great for storing water. However, you will want to make sure the jars are secure and don't fall to the ground. Old mayonnaise jars, pickle jars, and typical canning jars can all be useful storage containers.

How to Find It, Disinfect It, and Purify It

Okay, you couldn't or didn't store enough water to last you as long as the power grid failure. That means you are in a bit of a bind and you need to find water—fast. So, before you head out into the great outdoors in the search of water, you need something to put it in. If you can't store water, you can at least keep a few jugs or other vessels on hand to carry the water in after you find it.

How to Find It

Have you ever heard about a snowball (or other substances) rolling downhill? The same can be said of water. It will always flow downhill. When you are in the search for water, you need to use all of your senses and common sense is one of them. Listen for water. When you hear the tell-tale signs, start heading towards it and ensure you're going down. Use your nose to smell rot caused by wetness. You can smell wet foliage. Find a vantage point that will allow you the best view of your surroundings. Look for greenery. Green indicates growth, which requires water. The water may not be immediately visible. You may need to do a bit of digging to find the water, but it is there.

Trees can also point you in the right direction. There are some trees that will only thrive with a steady source of water. If you see one of these (you will need to do your homework and research the trees so you can identify them), you will know water is around. The following trees are water lovers:

Above image shows how to extract water from trees using a clear plastic bag

- Cypress
- Willow
- Sycamore
- White birch
- White oak

When you are looking for water, it is important to find a source that is within a few miles of where you are living. Walking too far is going to zap you of your strength and you can't afford that to happen. If your power grid fails in the summertime, you could end up getting dehydrated from the lack of water while searching for more water.

Some other places you can find water are as follows:

- swimming pools
- hot tubs
- hot water heaters

- rivers
- lakes
- ponds
- streams
- rock crevices
- muddy ground

Nature is full of hiding places for water. We humans will struggle to find the water, but animals have an instinct and will act as your guide. You can use a number of different animals to find water. Check out some of these following methods:

- Birds circling an area means water is present.
- Bees will fly in a line towards a water source.
- Heavy bug activity indicates water is close.
- Animal tracks will lead you to water.

If you are still struggling to find water, you can collect dew and moisture. Bags tied around brush or leafy limbs will collect dew. It won't be a lot of water, but if you have several bags and plenty of green vegetation, you can get enough water to sustain you. Use a cotton towel, t-shirt, or other piece of fabric to wipe the front lawn early in the morning. You can collect the dew and wring out the cloth into a bowl. Collecting dew works best when there is high temperatures during the day and cool temperatures at night.

For winter situations, you can melt snow. However, to get an inch of water, you will need anywhere from three to five inches of snow depending on the moisture content of the snow. Do your best to collect clean snow. Listen to your mother's advice and avoid the yellow snow.

Desert situations can use solar stills if water is simply not available. This will require a lot of patience with very little water being put out. Some water is better than no water. Making a solar still is something every prepper should learn to do. Solar still making is fairly simple and you don't really need any tools.

Purifying Water

The universal rule in survival is all water is dirty and unsafe to drink. Although that crystal clear mountain stream may look clean, it is likely loaded with viruses and bacteria that can make you extremely sick. Animals are not bothered by the idea of drinking water they stand in and use the bathroom in. Dead animals lie in the water causing all kinds of pollutants to spread throughout the water. Humans are not always the best stewards and are known to dirty up water supply systems as well. Never risk drinking water that isn't purified.

You risk developing serious illnesses that can cause diarrhoea, vomiting, muscle weakness, and severe stomach pain. These things lead to dehydration. Don't risk it. Never drink dirty water unless it is an absolute emergency.

You will find there are filters and purifiers on the market. They are not the same. The best you are going to find are purifiers that offer 99.9 percent removal rate. There is no guarantee every little bit is going to be removed.

Filters remove bacteria and debris from the water. They tend to leave the water tasting a little better and leave it clear. They **DO NOT** remove all viruses. There are some filters that are better than others. The trick is to look at the smallest micron it can catch in the filter. The smaller it can capture, the better the purifier will work.

Purification methods remove bacteria and viruses. The methods involve chemicals purifying the water. The water is often left with a chlorine taste and smell.

Here are some of the nasty bugs that could be hiding in the water you collect.

Cryptosporidium- Product in human and animal waste; boiling water is about the only way to kill the dangerous protozoa. Chemical treatment alone will not kill cryptosporidium. A combination of chemical treatment i.e. iodine or bleach and filter will remove the majority of the cryptosporidium.

Giardia lamblia- Product of human and animal waste; boiling and filtering are the most effective ways of removing the parasite. Chemical treatment is only moderately effective except when using chlorine dioxide(water purification tablets). Combining filtering and chemical treatment removes the majority of the parasite from the water.

Salmonella- Found in faecal waste of humans and animals; boiling water is effective at removing the majority of the virus. Filters are only moderately effective. Chemical treatments have the highest rate. A combination of filtering and chemical treatment is the best bet.

E coli- Found in human and animal waste in the water; boiling water or using chemical treatment is the most effective method of removing the virus. Filtration has very limited removal rates.

Enterovirus, Rotavirus, Hepatitis A- Can cause typical stomach problems along with hepatitis and meningitis. Viruses are found in human and animal waste. Filtration has almost no possibility of removing these potentially deadly viruses from the water. Chemical disinfection or boiling the water is the most effective way to kill the viruses.

So, now that you know all the nasty bugs that could be lurking in your water, how do you clean it?

Boiling

Boiling water is considered the best option. However, when you are dealing with a downed power grid situation, that can make it a bit difficult. If you don't have a Coleman stove, a place to make a fire, or sterno heating cans, you will need to use chemical purification and filters.

While boiling water is the most popular way of killing bacteria the energy consumed to do this in a grid down situation can cause concern

To clean water via boiling, you need to let the water come to a rolling boil. You don't need to boil the water for five minutes. Once you see a nice rolling boil, remove the water from the heat to prevent it from evaporating. The water then is considered safe to drink.

Chemical Treatment

Chemical treatment can be done several different ways. ensure you store enough chemicals to treat your water. Remember, one gallon of water per day, per person. A short-term grid failure could leave you without power for 30 days. Always err on the side of caution and store extra. It is better to have and not need, than to need and not have.

Tablets

The most effective method of chemical treatment is the tablets you find in the camping section of the store. These are usually sold with 30 tablets in a bottle. You typically need one tablet for every gallon of water but the bottle should provide that information as well. Tablets are sold with either an iodine or chlorine chemical purification solution. The chlorine dioxide tablets are the only ones effective at killing the majority of the viruses that may be found in water.

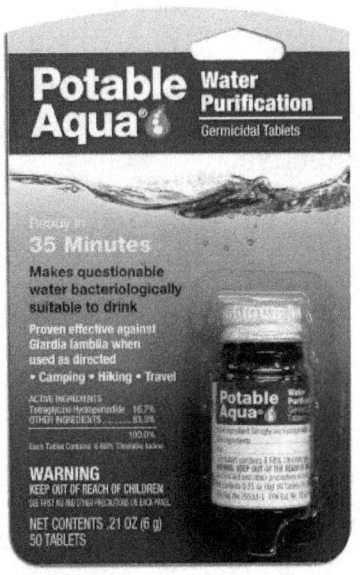

Iodine tablets are not as effective. There is also the risk of somebody being allergic to the iodine. Anybody with a shellfish allergy will likely be allergic to iodine. Tablets are an easy way to take care of purifying your water. When you are on the move or don't have a way to boil the water, these are your best bet.

Chlorine Bleach

Bleach is often a prepper's plan for purifying water. However, bleach has a very short shelf life and only lasts about 6 months. If this is going to be your purification method, you have to stay on top of the rotation of your supplies. Chlorine bleach is not effective at removing all viruses and bacteria. According to the CDC, it is only moderately effective.

The following chart will help you determine how much bleach you

need to purify your water.

Volume of Water to be Treated	Bleach Solution to Add
1 quart/1 litre	5 drops
1/2 gallon/2 quarts/2 litres	10 drops
1 gallon	1/4 teaspoon
5 gallons	1 teaspoon
10 gallons	2 teaspoons

Bleach is a favourite among preppers because it is extremely cheap and a little goes a long way. If you are going to rely on bleach as your water purification method, it would be best if you ran it through a filter to catch any other remaining particles.

Iodine

Iodine is an option and some use it because it is in the household's designated medical kits already. Iodine is sold in much smaller bottles, which makes it great for those on the move. The iodine is light sensitive and must be stored in dark bottles out of the sunlight. To purify water, you need 5 drops for every quart of water or 20 drops for a gallon. Iodine is more expensive than bleach, which is why most preppers are not fond of using it as a water purification method.

Filters

There are numerous brands of filters available on the market today. As mentioned earlier, choose a filter with the smallest pore size. A .02 or .01 is your best bet. Another factor to consider when you choose a filter as your water cleaner is how many gallons

of water the filter clean before it is no longer effective. Filters are much more expensive than chemical purification methods, but you can typically clean more water with a filter than you can with a single bottle of chemical tablets. There are portable filters that look like straws, large filters you can set up in your home or medium-size filters that are portable, but are not quite as small as the straws. Make sure you store extra filters if you are buying one of the larger devices.

UV Filters

UV filters are an effective, yet pricey way to purify your water. UV filters can remove the majority of viruses, bacteria, and protozoa. There are portable devices as well as larger devices that can be kept in your home to purify larger amounts of water. You will need to have extra batteries on hand to use  your UV filtering system. There are some that are solar-charged and some that are a crank style system which are used to operate the filter.

Chapter 4
Sanitation
Toilets/Latrines, Hand Washing, Dishes, Bathing, and Trash

One of the biggest hurdles you will face in a downed power grid situation is sanitation. Filth is one way to get sick. There are reasons we have septic systems, sanitation systems, and trash pick-up. Without these things, are streets and towns would be riddled with human waste that would attract rodents and spawn disease. Sanitation must be taken very seriously. It isn't about sweeping the floors or dusting, it is about taking great care in keeping your home sanitary to avoid spreading disease.

We will cover each area of sanitation and how you can go about staying sanitary and as clean as possible without electricity.

Toilets

You need to plan your toilet use carefully. Without power, it won't be long before city sanitation systems go down. Use the toilet as you would until it is no longer an option. If you live on land with your own well and you have an electric pump, you are not going to have the option of using your toilet unless you have a generator powerful enough to run your pump. If you have an abundance of water, like you live next to a river or have a big swimming pool in the backyard, you could manually flush the toilet. Conserve water and only flush a few times throughout the day, unless it is necessary to flush more often.

You can create a makeshift toilet in your bathroom by flushing the toilet until the bowl is empty of water. Place a heavy-duty garbage bag in the toilet. It doesn't hurt to double bag it. Use the toilet as you would normally. Change the bag at least every day or more often as needed. Place the bag outside immediately. It is best to bury the bag of waste in a hole that is at least 8 inches deep and 200 feet away from any water sources. If you don't want to use the toilet in the house, a 5-gallon bucket can be used in the same fashion.

Digging a hole that is 8 to 12 inches deep outside is also an option. Once you have used the hole, fill it in and place rocks or heavy branches over the area. Animals will be attracted to the area and will attempt to dig it up.

Hand-Washing

You will need to be extra vigilant about keeping your hands clean when there is no power. Hot water is not going to be readily available. Soap is going to be an absolute must. Water will also be in short supply so you cannot afford to waste it.

Pour a little water on your hands and add soap. Wash your hands thoroughly for at least 20 seconds. Pour a little more water over your hands to rinse off the soap. Use hand sanitizer after washing for an added layer of protection. Wash your hands throughout the day as you normally would. Wash after using the bathroom, changing the toilet bag, or handling trash. You cannot afford to get sick. Teach your children the hand washing procedure as well. Keep a good supply of anti-bacterial soap on hand so you don't have to skimp. Don't bother with the pretty smelling soap. Go for the stuff that works.

Dishes

Unless you have stocked up on paper plates and disposable cutlery, you are going to have to wash dishes. That means you are going to have to do it the old fashioned way— without a dishwasher. You need to use purified water to wash your dishes with. Don't use water that isn't clean as you could end up spreading viruses to your plates, which then when you eat off those

Having a ready supply of disposable crockery and cutlery can be useful as it you help you conserve water

plates, you'd end up getting sick. You can certainly use water that hasn't been purified to rinse the dishes before putting them into a sink of soapy water. Heat water whenever possible to use for your dishwashing needs.

Bathing

Daily hot showers are probably not going to be possible. Bathing is a luxury, but in a situation where you have very little water, it is not quite as important to take a shower and wash your hair every day. You do, however, need to stay clean. Sponge baths are important. They will make you feel better while removing sweat and dirt that has accumulated throughout the day.

Investing in a camp shower today can make you a whole lot happier in the event you do lose power. The showers are hung up outside or in a window. The sun heats the water which is going to give you the luxury of water pouring over your body. A trick to conserve water while still enjoying the feel of water falling over you is to turn on the water enough so you are wet. Turn it off and lather up. Turn on the water again and rinse quickly. You can take a nice, almost warm shower with just a couple gallons of water.

One bit of personal hygiene you don't want to skimp on is brushing your teeth. Use only purified water to do this. Put the toothpaste on your brush and brush your teeth. Use a few sips of water to rinse and spit. Don't waste water by dipping your toothbrush into the water or drinking a big gulp of water that you are going to spit out anyway.

Trash

Trash that is left to accumulate will stink up your house and invite unwanted guests like ants, mice, and roaches. Tossing the trash outside isn't a good idea either. You are inviting much bigger pests to hang out in your front yard. If the power grid is only down for a few days, you don't have much to worry about. If the grid is down for more than a week, sanitation trucks are not going to be able to get the gas they need to drive around collecting trash. You are going to need to take care of it yourself.

Recycle what you can. Smash down boxes and cans to reduce the amount of space needed to store your trash. If you are sure the trash service will be running within a couple of weeks, you could store your trash inside bins with lids set away from your house. If the grid is going to be down any longer than that, you need to find a better option for disposing of your trash.

You can burn paper products. Avoid burning plastic if possible. This releases noxious chemicals into the air. Plastics are recyclable in most cases. Put them to the side to be recycled later.

If you can't burn your garbage, bury it. You will need to bury it at a depth that allows at least 12 inches of dirt over the top of it. Animals will be attracted to your garbage. Place rocks or heavy branches over the area to deter them from digging it up and creating a mess.

Store your garbage as far from your house as possible. Use heavy-ply garbage bags to prevent the bags from deteriorating and making a stinky mess. If you live in a neighbourhood, talk with your neighbours about designating a place for trash to be stored until it can be collected. The area should be as far from water sources and homes as possible.

Chapter 5
Cooking, Cooling, Lighting, and Heating
How to Maintain a Healthy Environment

Basic things like staying warm, getting out of the heat, or cooking a meal are things we take for granted. When the power grid fails, you are going to learn in a hurry how much we rely on electricity to fill those needs. You need to have alternatives in order to be healthy.

Cooking

You have to eat and eating cold canned food day in and day out for weeks will get old, really quick. In fact, you could actually develop something known as food fatigue. Food fatigue will wreak havoc on your digestive system. You will suffer from diarrhoea, vomiting and stomach cramps. You need to be able to change up your diet to avoid food fatigue.

Vintage wood stoves like this were designed when there was no grid so they can not only heat your home and cook your food but some of them also feature wet backs which can provide you with a constant supply of hot water

Cooking food is actually one of the least of your problems when the power is out. A fire-pit in the backyard, your barbecue, or a camp stove can all be used to heat your food. You can prepare soup, stews, and even casseroles when you have a source of heat. Take the time to invest in at least one of the above methods to heat your food. Buy cast iron cookware that will withstand the heat of an open fire.

Stock up on foods that you can throw in a heavy pot and hang over an open fire. Freeze-dried meals are great and don't require any actual cooking. However, you will need water and a way to heat the water.

You will want to invest in some manual kitchen tools as well. Things like a manual can opener, manual hand mixer, or a hand-crank blender all come in handy when you want to mix up a meal without electricity. Don't forget a percolator to make your morning cup of coffee.

Cooling

It may not seem like one of those priorities you want to put at the top of your list, but hyperthermia is just as dangerous as hypothermia. You have to keep your body at a safe temperature to avoid heatstroke or heat exhaustion.

You can keep your home cool or at least relatively comfortable without electricity. You will need to cover all of the windows with blankets or heavy curtains. Block out the sun. Keep the windows closed as well if the outside temperature is high. You don't need the hot air coming in to the house. If you have a basement, stay in the area, which will be naturally cooler.

Avoid cooking indoors or running excessive lights. You don't want to produce any unnecessary heat. Do your best to leave the majority of the chores to the late night or early morning hours to avoid overheating. If your home doesn't have any trees or a way to get any shade, you may be better off taking shelter under a tree.

Heating

Keeping your house warm is a bit of a bigger challenge than keeping it cool if you do not have an alternate source of heat. A woodstove is your best bet. When the power does come back on, you will be able to use your woodstove to augment your heating bill. It is a way to cook your food, dry your clothing, and can provide light. If it is possible,

A simple wood heater like this is a great investment as it can be a great way to save money on gas or electricity if the grid works well BUT if the grid does go down it can be used to heat your home and with a little improvisation can be used to cook with and boil drinking water

make the investment and have a woodstove installed in your home.

You can also stay warm by closing all the doors in the house to cut down on unnecessary drafts. If the temperatures are really cold, huddle in a single, small room. Body heat will keep you and your family warm.

Cover the windows and doors with heavy drapes or blankets. Roll up towels and place them underneath the doors to block drafts. You can further cut down on drafts by taping plastic over the windows and using duct tape to hold it in place. If you have a south facing window and the sun is bright, leave it uncovered and allow the sun to warm the room.

Never use gas heaters or put a generator inside the home to try and stay warm. This can cause carbon monoxide poisoning. Burning candles serves a dual purpose, it provides you with light while producing some heat.

Lighting

Sitting in the dark for hours on end can wreak havoc on your mental state. You need to have light to cook by, read by, and to provide you with a sense of safety and security. You have a number of options to getting light into your home and quite frankly, it is the easiest task you have in your preparation for a grid failure.

Flashlights are great for walking around the house or checking on things outside. Opt for LEDs that require less battery power and are brighter in general. Make sure you have plenty of backup batteries.

Solar powered garden lights can make great affordable indoor lights as they can be charged up during the day and brought| indoors at night

Lanterns are an excellent option for lighting up a large area. There are battery-powered lanterns and lanterns that are solar-charged. Solar lanterns are a better option because they don't require you to keep a large supply of D-batteries on hand.

Emergency candles are an option, but it is important you are careful not leave them unattended. Make sure you have adequate candle holders on hand that will support the emergency candles. Candles in jars will suffice, but they do not put out as much light as taper candles.

The inexpensive solar lights you put in your garden and along your pathway make excellent indoor lights as well.

Set the lights outside during the day and bring them in at night. This is one situation where you could use solar lights as a night light all night long. There are numerous styles with some offering more light than others. Browse your home and garden store and choose a few that you can bring inside.

Chapter 6
Strategies to Help You Properly Manage Your Resources in the Event of a Grid Down Emergency

You have to manage your supplies and resources because you cannot possibly know for sure when the power will come back on. If you were caught off guard and have limited supplies you need to be especially careful with how you use them.

It is going to take a lot of self-control. You can't flip on the flashlight and leave it on as a night light. You can't toss out the water at the bottom of the cup because you don't want it. Eating until you are bloated is also not an option.

The following are some strategies to help you manage what you have:

- When the grid fails, it is time to take inventory of what you have on hand. What you have is all you are going to have for the duration.

- Portion out the water for each family member. You need to make sure everybody is getting what they need to survive, without wasting resources.

- Instruct each member of the family about the importance of conserving things like toilet paper, toothpaste, candles, and battery power.

- If your supplies are in an open area, move them to a space that can be secured. You want to keep them out of sight to avoid tempting those who didn't prepare.

- Eat the food in your refrigerator and freezer first and save your canned and freeze-dried foods for the coming weeks.

- Fill your tub and every available pot the moment the power goes out. This will give you a head start on the water situation. The water you draw will be safe to drink and will not need further purification.

- Organize your supplies so you can more readily find what you need and how much you have on hand. You don't want to be checking the pantry, the basement, and under the bed for your supplies. Group like items together.

- Check expiration dates and move items that expire first to the front.

Staying calm is the key to managing your supplies. When you panic, you are prone to burn through your resources or end up hurting yourself by not using them as they needed. Planning ahead will help you keep a cool head in true survival situation.

Conclusion

A power grid failure is something that can and will likely happen. The extent of the failure is anybody's guess. You need to be prepared for it all. If the power outage only extends a few days, you are in luck. Consider it a training period. It is a good chance to see how well you prepared. Take note of the things that didn't go well and figure out ways to make it better.

You must start your preparations today. Waiting until it happens will be too late. You will be one of the ones left pounding on neighbour's doors asking for help. There is a pretty good chance the doors will be slammed in your face or possibly not opened to begin with. Don't put it off. Start doing what you can to prepare your family for a power grid failure.

From The Author

Thank you for taking the time to read this book. As an author, I understand the importance of creating books which my readers will find both enjoyable and informative. If you have the time and feel generous, please don't hesitate to leave an honest review of this book..........Ron Johnson

Other Books By Ron Johnson

Prepper's Pantry

In the event of an emergency having an adequate supply of food could mean the difference between life and death!

Are you prepared for any disaster that is about to happen? Do you already have emergency supplies? Is it enough to sustain you and your family's life for an extended period, when help from others would be close to impossible? Have you discussed and implemented the emergency plans with your family?

Fighting for your survival during times of disaster is not about luck, it's about the right knowledge that will help you pull through it. It is all about saving you and your family's life, with the tips provided in this book. Guess what? YOU CAN MAKE IT HAPPEN by reading and following all the guidelines laid out in my book.

RV Living For Beginners

Are You Fed Up Of Working The 9-5 To Pay The Mortgage Or Rent Plus The Bills And Considering Leaving It All Behind And Hitting The Road?

When you want to change your lifestyle entirely, you need to have enough motivation but you also need to have knowledge about the lifestyle that you are adopting. Many people who want to live in an RV full-time fail to find a balance in their lives which make that living pleasurable, while others can live the dream and learn to compromise on comforts for the sake of freedom. They wake up in the mornings to feel that they have breathed fresh air. They see different scenery every morning if they so wish. What you need to know before joining them is whether you're cut out for the lifestyle and what differences there are between living in a conventional home and living in an RV. This book bridges that gap in your knowledge, and although you may choose to save a fortune by staying at home, you may also choose the lesser travelled road and discover the benefits of living in an RV.

Both lifestyles, either in an RV or a home, have their pros and cons. Many who choose the RV lifestyle find that adapting their lives comes naturally. It takes a unique and free spirited person to compromise on the luxuries of home living in favor of the adventurous lifestyle offered by RV living, though many do. Once you weigh the pros and cons, you can make the choice wisely, and that's what this book is all about. The book will appeal to the free spirited who seek something more than merely surviving month to month oppressed by bills, mortgage payments and housing taxes.

Both have benefits, though those who live the life they choose, rather than the life chosen for them by responsibility, find that RV life tests their personal boundaries and skills freeing up their lives to live beyond the grid. Journey with us and learn if living in an RV will suit you, and be prepared for the journey of your life.